Formido and Other Poems
Travis Emerson Gouré

In hoping these may resolve or clarify but some modest piece of my wretchedness:

For my Mother, Father, my Brothers, my only love Madison,

And for the unremittingly anxious. May it leave us all at once.

up

are you awake

I wanted
to wake you.

the thunder
leaked out
of the earth.

Now is
coming

Now is
coming

you are not awake
nothing is awake.
--I'll wake you.

with thunder that watches legislators and imperialists
creep into obscurity.

are you awake?

we have things to do
we have
guns to hold to our typewriters
to our hands
that they might be so moved
to manifest the miracle
of crushing out a place
for artistry
in Now's
inelegant
labyrinths.

I will wake you.
I will mend the decrepit god
and tremble in its depth

I will wake you,

for I must.

formido II

as you step
so it does
like Laelap

like a thing crying and lost

be sure

it will file and creep
until it has you
deep in a well
and drowned.

run and build
run
run
and build a stone
somewhere deep
in the ground

though unwanted, still at least
unfound.

mother

she keeps her kids in the dark
maybe
she cries in a white room
maybe she walks to a hotel
in a robe
paling

the one who's done herself in
the mother who's got to get
rid
of the germ
in her
 self

the mother who
can't drink
maybe

maybe she keeps a flask in the dresser

maybe she just takes pills.

maybe she just wants to
be clean.

who
is only herself
alone
and reads alone
destroys alone
she is most beautiful
midday
between her tired
and her fearful hours
slightly before the
heat
of the deep afternoon
when the world starts to quiet down
when she meditates on the consequence
of her interpretations
and the good
of other people

she is determined.

she is determined.
she keeps collages for old friends
everywhere in the living room
and wooden antiques
and postcards

it's a primitive sort of loveliness...
like always waking up.

maybe

she thinks the world is
unnerved
by her being
or that maybe she,
unnerved by the world
could have been the glistening thing in the warfield
taken up with the glory of being a thing
had not more wars came and rolled mud over those
most remarkable details

but no less
a kind of radiance which does not deserve
so much trouble,
and for which
she is iron.

my mother, my mother, the way I am now
how have you endured?

maybe she prays
maybe she prays all day
maybe she sits on white sheets
and makes again that gesture
of more

and has written it down before
but it's muddled

maybe

we aren't looking right

such a woman never did add up
her just woes

to this

oh that I weren't such trouble
with more to come, in blinding regiments
all at once starving and pounding the heart
while they watch me sleeping on the floor
pills beside
love beside
guild beside
oh, that I weren't so much for you my mother

maybe she messed up.
maybe she messed up
once.

and lost all that she loved
long
long
ago.

formido I

the cold measures of horror
bitter as poor
rise as from a numb sleep
counting up the grey beams of light
one, two and three into late fall
and it's raining

and ringing

and we tilt
and we slide
out of time

like war mounds in a storm.

into the dread
of the ache
of any
honorable
life

and remembering
the unease
of being
at all...

where now
the eyes are treacherous to the heart,
and the hands in dismay
at their own gross abilities.

god or no god
whiskey or pills
ceiling tiles and Salinger.

what sorrow brings us to...

what death brings to us,

and what an oddity
is excellence
in
this

life.

formido IV

where is the fear
there is the dread
in a weary dark

though their bodies
too bleak
in architecture
rest like frightened
soldiers
and render existence in smoke
and tired shades.

it is an unknowable breath
in a vague reply

it is an unspeakable
bit of earth
toiled by
some cross and awful mechanic
unheld by the cages of god
who will speak to no one
of its nature.

look,
if you will
you can:

in the redbreast on
the porch in the dim colors of
the morning
the delicate breath from our mouths in the cold
just
before the faces
the responsibilities
the
scared encounters

and waiting.

there:

the dread
and anxious
hours

spent drinking in
the basement
with Kafka
and poetry
there:
old and trembling
looking
for the bottles in
the cabinet
or young and silent
chewing up the stale beatings
from father

there

the still and forgotten
the bugs in the wool
in the rain
in fog

in prisons.

there is their birthmother
the demon feeling
the common murderer
as reasonless
as a heaven
and the astonishing claim it has to me
is as deep and empowered
as revolt

so I must live to kill it
or let it stretch my skin around verandas of hell
now we know
what man is against himself
which created history
and plagued the beauty
requested of our gods.

formido V

in the course of fear
is the thing itself

in the footprint
is the poison

with no opposite
and a nameless
grieving history
in the heart.

the anxious
are logicians of fear

they draw the lines
of its veins
in their spare hours, and try devise
its form
unconsciously.

but all of our suppositions cannot stand within it.
they are fatally cracked by its incertitude.

we are in its hands.
we are in its home.

How it happened

A panel of ravens to make statements against the thinker.
Sitting on existence, the ugly building…set like masters, they say:
'Don't sit and watch him crack his beads forever,
He only forgets…then forgets again.'

And from all the great departments of the world
Is laughter, finally the good King has made Goliath of the intellect,
David of the doing, who will overcome with the hands
That choke the child.

We are now at the throats of brass tax, and proofs
from ancient figureheads. It is all we can think about.
Everywhere our poets are swallowing the deskwood
With fistfuls of Queen pennies, sitting in drivel.

And if what comes next are visitations from monsters
That you see in the longest cars, with the prettiest voices
Decrepit mercenaries wheeling along glass children,
These are artists, turned over to the worst of affluence.

Rilke said

Rilke said to be patient

when the mind becomes such the library that Borges
kept up in...
and allow
a mere
(name
like a face
on a counterfeit
check)
hope

to outfit
this
agonizing gesture of being.

I can't yet imagine it
I can't yet calm this shaking
or I cannot
disseminate my will
unto such old
bronze
stances.

the Thinker could never so.

and his endless
disquieted place
is a writ
of sickness
that I have felt with
nearly as much
permanence

on the days which
like printed
newspaper
read
one way
and arrive
at the doorstep
each and every time,
even
with the news so

sad and horrid.
I cannot yet be patient
without too being mad
this Babyl perpetuates a frightened breath
where each of my essences
hide.

and nothing will give me time.
no one will give me time
no one will give me time.

blue pills and Prokofiev

only do that dance which makes you tired
only do that dance which makes you sweat
there is no use in melancholy:
they cannot find us tonight.

celebrate now
so tap the earth as Argentinean feet
on the rooftops in Paris in the 60s

the rooftops in Paris
where the sky cries its histories.

only drink that cup which makes you drunk
only drink that cup which makes you smile
there is no use in anguish:
they won't find us
tonight
they can't find us
tonight.

so celebrate
kiss the dirt with Italian bounty
in the graveyards of lovers young

the graveyards of young lovers
where the sky sleeps for centuries.

<u>formido VI</u>

be it trouble or disease or death
we wait for it

rarely independent
of it

not often
out of sight
from the wounding coercion
of the heart
ever ever

ever toward

the origin
of this
attenuated living.

formido VIII

it doesn't matter how many women
I get to fuck, I say,
this kid says 'I got 12'

two cigarettes
and the evening becomes blue

it will make the same sound
that old sound
off through the window
in the same tired city
as in the angry houses down
the street
where the husband pulls
the knife and says

for the last time

for the last

the last
god
damn
time...

it
wouldn't matter
how many episodes of beauty
I am given
it would build no less unto
dark theatres
walking bodies dimming
with the day
and where the water in the street
the light of
the crowd
all the living mercenaries
of imitation
breath
and make the music which disturbs me.

and it wouldn't matter
where I go
I'm not getting away.

I don't have a thing to do
but things to do for everyone.

but I carry
the last time,
I carry it.
the last time

the last
god damn
time
that the night takes hold
of my bedroom
and I stand in the gloom
like some lover gone away.

The City

the
 self
was lost
in Platonic unity,
and since,
no one has adequately
given it
a home
in their philosophy

the city
is the piece
that turns the self
astray,
a city that
rests on
after all
bitter
unions

and later
there is a sort of
anger
in its necessities
as it appears
there must be a strong
and a less strong
to delineate the
means
of existing.

and then the city
is a watchtower
or the city is a king,
darkening
and growing
louder as he's frightened
by the duplicity he
can't
rub from his
face

and the markets
are on fire

and the land is
used up
and the histories
continue on
into
other
black
books
getting smaller
and smaller.

state
philosophy for now
has the mind.

the search is for
the
 self.

formido XII

diffused by movement
dissolved by touch
and buried by voice
it is the impossible
that will ravage
until the cold heart goes

white

in a matter of time
in a matter of time
skin of liminality:
the body of a dead thing
yet a living beast
in the Self's
suffered wilderness.

which now a drowned
conundrum
with cities
for teeth
and towers
warring for
symbolism

le nouvelle guerre
has iron seams
with no escapes
and without tragic
burden:
for it is the pressure of
the eternal man
so did nation
create hell on earth.

more and more
irreparable in structure
are those magnificent cathedrals I used to kiss
and I step away
further
further
off.

it is a kind of dread

which needs first
to know the blood
of that it cradles
with the palm of a lilac that
eats you as you sleep
and cradles
cradles,
murderous
but
forever
giving.

Formido XX

formido is the distance from the horror
between the tremor
and swelling
of the stomach that ties
in its multiplicities
to your ligaments
and your efforts
and the world stares wildly
at your
animal movements.

formido is the stain
on the person
ignored and always known
unspeakably resented
disquieting moments

in the sun deep in my face
and the darkness
deep in my Self
and our selves
away from our
joie de réalité
for this
dynamic ambiguity
rattles in the spine of each
unhappy man,
that he
who searches for the heart of the thing
will after all lose his head
to this leviathan of the
thoughts.

<u>mantra</u>

there are only so many things
this body
can do
only so
much
this body
can do

it will never
be the best at
anything
I suppose
this is the way
people die

they notice
day by day

that they weren't
the
one
for this
or that
and
tomorrow then
is already bruised
by the night
and night despised
by
morning blue

there are only
so many things
the light can help you
imagine.

only so
much
this world
can show you,

we realize
time
and again

time
is a foolish thing to attach
to life
we'd do better
to conceive the world
as unreal
and ourselves
as gods of
some space
at least…

no matter
how little
or how strange.

<u>another one for the deep</u>

all the souls I see are good
but I don't see many
none truly
as yet
I suppose
a nod to
the poets of faith

I guess
too much of the geist

artists and industrialists
blindly intertwined
with courts and prisons limitless
and monsters and heroes
too frequently the same.

there has never been such a thing called
passion
in capitalist projects

there was soul in the fight for our nation
but not in its paperwork
not in its modernity

yes, the courage of human action
has made me weep
uncommon strength
among horrid voices
and those who
make you desire
more of life
but it seems
these more
fortuitous
souls see
no world of daedal threads
but only the cold ends
tragedy
and purity
wherein we rise like a kingdom
out of wars
hells
crucifixions

and at last it seems
that human decision
and transgression
is ultimate
in the nature
of earth

but so many
silent anxieties
so many
empty
wordless terrors
as small as grain
as tired and reposed
as smoke
slide and tilt through our eyes
the quietly grieving inertia
in the anguished breath
of this endeavor
this
misstep...
existence.

<u>For David Foster Wallace, for whom it was too much</u>

Oh, the awes of evil
And the image of goodness worn
In the passions of fear.

For whom beauty blinds
There are always dimmer roses,
Did you know this as you went
to die?

You knew us
Crippled thinkers
Still-life kids
Leaning in these weak, protean passages
And grotesque threads

You knew
To dissimilate
Is only done
At gunpoint

Nor to gather up
The newly conquered
With an angry voice
If not
To have them
Break your neck when first they
Can

I don't know what all you knew
But I have to think about it
I can only do
Heavily
Permanently
Tired
Pressed in this seat
Shattered by my city
Shattered by my nation...

And can't end up like you,
For no one would allow it.

I give my night

I'll give my night away to this
I've forgotten how one sleeps.

I'm filled with smoke and receding.

receding.

I'm stepping back
out of something
terrifying

like I always do.

like I pound my head
and give up.

the couch
with the bottles
emptying again
the drugs
on the carpet
and coffee table…
the thorough loneliness
in a form of light

I give my night
away to this.

swallowing down
whatever it is

madness and liquor
powder and silence

I wish that
I knew what it was
I was doing
when the sun keeps
resting
and my eyes don't close
even
my mother's wine
is gone in me

but the world is as concrete
as a sacrifice.

some primitive and blank stillness
which cannot war with melancholy:
one cannot war with abstractions
they are devils with eyes like comfort
and I've tried

on these twilights
laughing
through the sinking moments
pouring Nothing down my throat,
but am as grey and sore a man
as a statue built to grieve.

I only sit,
speaking with the children of fear,
discarding my moments to them
and breathing
their desultory answers
their windowless frameworks of living.

I give my night away to this.

ordered confessional

man is lonely in the rain
and the rain of time
smiles lush
knocking about
in the grains of history's
workings.

father I feel this is a needle
dragging dull patterns to life
only

only an old
discarded fabric
used to clean the blood
of spirit

I'd prefer to be
empty
in its view
though it knows
I hide that livid god in
my breast
who accepts nothing
but renewal.

oh

that I could go unseen
in the thick dreams of beauty's disassembly

I am another figure
in modernity's lightning film

of grinning dust.

and god made me
a writer
and so is cruel,

there in a laughable
kingdom
of ceaseless mishap
and architectured flowers.

there is something
about our carrying on
in this earth
which rots
the mechanisms of beauty
in whomever's art
we will be said
to have been in
at the end of this
raw, crass
road.

formido XVII

my god is called Proteus

I am an unwillingly
reverenced
script.

he touches nothing
though all things
like a breaking mirror
become my pieces
and his pieces

are as dead
as violent

as cracked
as seamless

at once
a wall which dissolves
a sea
which crumbles

it has made my kisses
ardent
and afraid
it has made the rainstorm awful
and superb
it has made the earth a heaven
and a stone.

I am the writ
of a fastened silence
the crypt
of his lightless home

I have that feeling which does not sleep
I have that god named madness.
I have that god named Proteus.

Have I escaped

still I dreamt of being hit by cars
and immobilized for months:

the hospital a heavy sighing machine
bitterness so distinguished
on the outset of each
drying mouth,
and the looming beauty of hysteria
on the faces of
young daughters.

I am the orderly's favorite.
cordial and quiet.
and with a shy face…

'pour moi,' she insists.

while with my skin
still smooth in places
and my face
more unscathed at least than
a burn victim:
all the world is certain
I was beautiful
and tried
and worried much
and feared
everything

before some dumb luck
left me limbless in the ward
doing nothing
and with nothing
to do, feeling only
my head sway
back and
forth

in rhythms of Mendelssohn

as I sleep,
wake
and smile
to the ceiling

what a god
my god.

to effect calm at the dawn of my unraveling
to quiet
the old body:
that rendering of a storm as when storms depict
the hellish abilities
of earth to choke men.

but rather
I'm a talented listless idiot
with such, such
potential

potential has the same name as morning.

I sit
as in the other listless artist's homes,
gravely mechanical
decaying beneath the rouge…

god does not
unclothe the wind
but you and me instead
in the view of a distorted mountain
where each royal of our consciousness stands
with the tyrants of our misgivings.

The nature of winter

those who have stepped
between the flowers of winter
between
the brutes of trepidation
and the sky of our
languid god
plain as a supposition
know

the delicacy of morality
the reasoning
of kings
and the heritages
of so many bleeding prisoners.

they know
the vital interpreter,
the precedents
of speech…
the necessity of the knife
in the left hand
of the criminal
and the vile
in the right.

we who have
crawled through the homes of the perverse
careful as a hiding child
and watched their arts…
who have
deliberated with ice
kissed stillness
and experienced Nothing
know all of earth and thought
can melt into the deep

each daedal line can settle
in the folds of the rose
and the pockets of the iris
in the pool
on the lily
crossing
over
the bodies.

somewhere
there is a haven
for each trace of existing:

the marigolds insist.
the hydrangeas insist.
the trees insist.

the seasons demand.

but the creator was a poor writer.
disparate, and cold.
and was overcome with panic
when he fashioned the leaves.

so all the lengths of nature grew
irrevocably and loudly.

now everywhere we render
the soul to a branch
or justice to an oak.

so lawmakers and fascists do
intolerance to scriptures
ignorance to upbringing.

and that is the misgiving of the King
which is the oldest thing.

his Eden failed conceive
the tyranny of leaves,
for Eden wasn't holy,
but a pose.

<u>Dear God</u>

where the first notion was life
the second was excess.
lies, speeches,
buildings and burials.

history, if a montage of the insatiable,
is also the spectacle of angels.

The Morning After

The man rises, spreads;
Blending eyes,
The forest meets with a
Faced heart.
He feels alone
Moments before the flesh
Dispersed, and the unseeable pillar
Bore him in marble grain
He was cold.

The purple root goes unanswered as he passes.
It tightens its arch,
His feet break
Once more
The vulgar soil in his mouth.

Heaven's namelessness begins to give him headaches,
He notices the ground is very gray.

<u>the particulars</u>

hell
is this cold, low category
made up as a contrived
and bitter statue…
we are Michelangelo's captives
embedded
in sight
which suggests the thing
before it
has lived.

half engraved
in the doing
of life
half born
in the new world

we could be
the airs above the nations
forth from fingers of latent villains,
notions which
continue into
the soulless phenomena
of earth.

but we…
half viewed
in our skin
half held
in dark perspectives

half condemned
half liberated
grieved

poets
plants
prisoners…
governors…

we wish to live
unabridged
but the sky maintains us
in the order in which

we surrender to it.

<u>My baby</u>

my baby does the swing
but with a sadness
and the branches of her frames are melancholy. I don't
know what to do
I don't know what to say

she won't speak
at all, the young rose might
as well be stoned
and with
dried lips,

she won't
say a thing.

but I know she wants my life

all my life.
and I don't have a thing.

at best
this is one silent
field
and the marble cities which hide
in their burials grounds too have wanted
to break their own teeth
for all the things they've said...
so I won't say a thing.

while my baby does the swing
with smoke and air and dust
I drink the bourbon
and the liquor
drips softly from my collar while she sings

and I can't say a thing.

I have
a seat
for the art of some weeping quiltmaker

such is time, ringing
with the deep force
of a Vatican bell.

I have nothing even
to give away

but my baby wants my life.
all my life,
and I won't let her in.

<u>allevo I</u>

days when you miss
every shot you make.

days when you feel all right.
all right
and okay.

tonight
I'm okay.

once every few months
maybe
perhaps twice a year
they kneel

these frostbitten forms
dressed in
exasperated smiles
with strange
massless stones in their throats

kneel
to a sun
which doesn't pound their chest into bedlam
and the ceiling tiles no longer turn
so fast into Sirenic graves
as the blood empties out of
the cheeks.

on these days
we have even considered praying,
but held fast...
to authentically suffering,
and not suffering.

and the genuine
feeling
I get
in one sick spot
on the body
the one
I try
to rub out
second to second

as I wake for days more
and more
with this miserable condition
is gone
for a while

and I can
for a moment
do
my human motions
more
as a living work
of flesh
than a dramaturgy of stone.

on those days when I feel all right...those
old
days.

www.ingramcontent.com/pod-product-compliance
Lightning Source LLC
Chambersburg PA
CBHW060632030426
42337CB00018B/3319